Color Your Way to a Life You Love™

OVERCOME FEAR

A SELF-HELP ADULT COLORING BOOK FOR RELAXATION & PERSONAL GROWTH!

60 CALMING DESIGNS TO COLOR!
FLOWERS & NATURE
ANIMALS
MANDALAS
DOODLES & PATTERNS

ALPHA DOLL

COLOR YOUR WAY TO A LIFE YOU LOVE™: OVERCOME FEAR

**For information:
shellijohnson.com
alphadollmedia.com**

Copyright Notice and Disclaimers

This book is Copyright © 2018 Shelli Johnson (the "Author"). All Rights Reserved. Published in the United States of America. The legal notices, disclosures, and disclaimers within this book are copyrighted by the Internet Attorneys Association LLC and licensed for use by the Author in this book. All rights reserved.

No part of this book may be reproduced or transmitted in any form or by any means, electronic or mechanical, including photocopying, recording, or by an information storage and retrieval system — except by a reviewer who may quote brief passages in a review to be printed in a magazine, newspaper, blog, or website — without permission in writing from the Author. For information, please contact the Author at the following website address: shellijohnson.com/contact

For more information, please read the "Disclosures and Disclaimers" section at the end of this book.

First Paperback Print Edition, January 2018

Published by Alpha Doll Media, LLC (the "Publisher").

ISBN: 978-0-9747109-8-3

WELCOME TO THE COLOR YOUR WAY TO A LIFE YOU LOVE™ COLORING BOOK SERIES!

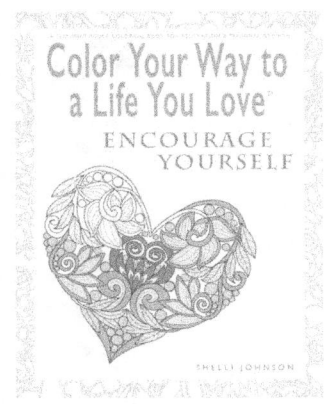  

AVAILABLE NOW OR COMING SOON!

UNLEASH YOUR INNER CREATOR & MAKE IT YOUR OWN!

This is not just another coloring book, it's also an invitation for you to delve deeper into who you are so you can find out what makes you come alive. I'm a big believer in the power of taking small steps to get you anywhere you need or want to go. With that in mind, I invite you inside these pages on a creative self-help adventure. You'll unleash your artistic side with designs and patterns while you do daily small-sized activities aimed at: 1. helping you heal yourself and 2. inspiring you to create a life you love. My hope is that you'll use these pages to ignite your imagination, discard your limitations, and free your inner creator.

Feel free to add your own personal embellishments to any image. You can make each page as unique as you like by adding doodles, patterns, and/or shapes. Color the images any way you like with any tools you like. There are no rules except that you relax, enjoy, and color in a way that feels right to you.

THE MEANING & PURPOSE OF LIFE!

"The meaning of life is to find your gift. The purpose of life is to give it away."
—Pablo Picasso

THE PSYCHOLOGY OF COLOR!

From my layman's understanding of the meaning of colors, certain colors can evoke certain emotions.

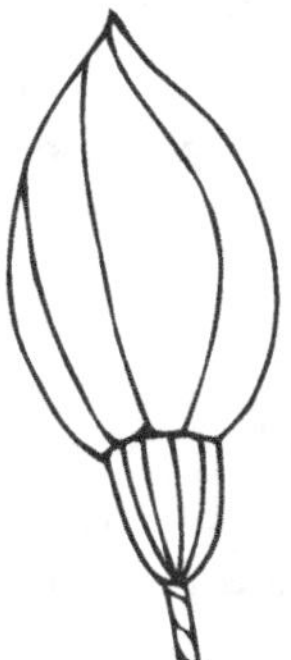

BLUE: centered, calm, hopeful, confidence
GREEN: growth, safety, endurance, calm
ORANGE: energy, happiness, encouragement, excitement
RED: passion, energy, strength, power, determination
YELLOW: joy, energy, cheerfulness
BROWN: stability
PURPLE: power, ambition, creativity, energy
BLACK: power, elegance, mystery
WHITE: light, goodness, safety

So keep that in mind as you color. If you're looking to experience a particular emotion/feeling/mood, you may want to use a particular color to help you get there.

A FEW HELPFUL SUGGESTIONS!

BABY STEPS
I'm a big believer in the power of taking baby steps to get you anywhere you need or want to go, which is why this coloring book is written the way it is. Each day has small-sized activities. They build on each other, one to the next. So feel free to color whichever image you'd like, just know you'll be best served to do the daily activities in order.

NO PERFECTION NEEDED
Do yourself a kindness and make a mistake in this coloring book early on. Scribble on some of the pages. Spill your favorite beverage on the cover. Rip one of the corners off. Color outside the lines. Make this book imperfect so that you'll feel free to be your real, honest self inside the pages. Being real, not being perfect, is what's going to heal you and set you free.

BE HONEST
I'd recommend that you don't show your answers inside this coloring book to anyone. Keep them to yourself for right now until you make it all the way through Day 30. Why? Honesty with yourself is what's going to help you heal and grow. You won't be completely honest if you're worried about someone reading your answers. In fact, what you're likely to do is tweak your responses, edit them, or scratch them out entirely if you're worried about how others might perceive you. So be kind to yourself & let this coloring book be just for you.

BE WILLING & OPEN
The first step to change is to be open & willing to it. You picked up this coloring book because you're struggling in this area of your life. If you want things to be different, well, both you & those things are going to have to change. So be open to experiencing something new & be willing to do the effort to get there.

GIVE YOURSELF PERMISSION
It's hugely important to give yourself permission (whether that's verbally or written) to: do the daily steps in this book, be/have/do/say/believe whatever you need to so that you can heal yourself, give yourself unlimited tries as many times as it takes, believe in your own worth and value, choose to create a life you love because you matter. Whenever you feel like you need someone else's permission to make a choice about your life, you just give that permission to yourself. The only permission you ever need to live your own life is your own.

YOU'RE ON A JOURNEY
It doesn't matter how old you are, how many times you've tried, or how far there is left to go. It's never too late to be the person you want to be. It's okay if you don't know things yet. You're on a journey and you'll figure it out as you go. This coloring book is designed to help you do just that.

BEGIN YOUR DAY WITH A STEP
If at all possible, do your daily step shortly after you wake up. That way, you'll be able to focus on yourself (because you're absolutely worth the time to do that) before your day gets away from you. So grab your favorite beverage. Find a quiet place. Relax and reflect while you're being creative.

IT'S A PRACTICE & A PROCESS
There's no doing this perfectly, and that's okay. You strive for progress. You do the best you can. So show yourself some patience and kindness because self-compassion is what you most need to heal yourself. You will make mistakes, there's just no way around it. Don't ever use any mistake as a reason to give up on yourself. Just circle back around and start again. And know this: every mistake is simply a brand new chance to do it better the next time.

AND FINALLY . . .
Remember (not just for this book but for all of life): you get out what you put in. So make yourself a priority in your own life because: 1. you're absolutely worth the effort and 2. no one else can do it for you. And one last suggestion good both for this book and for all of life: be brave and color outside the lines, that's where freedom lies.

THOSE WHO ARE BRAVE ARE FREE!

"It is not the critic who counts; not the man who points out how the strong man stumbles, or where the doer of deeds could have done them better. The credit belongs to the man who is actually in the arena, whose face is marred by dust and sweat and blood; who strives valiantly; who errs, who comes short again and again, because there is no effort without error and shortcoming; but who does actually strive to do the deeds; who knows great enthusiasms, the great devotions; who spends himself in a worthy cause; who at the best knows in the end the triumph of high achievement, and who at the worst, if he fails, at least fails while daring greatly, so that his place shall never be with those cold and timid souls who neither know victory nor defeat."

—Theodore Roosevelt

Source: excerpt (also known as *The Man In The Arena*) from the speech "Citizenship in a Republic" delivered at The Sorbonne in Paris, France on April 23, 1910.

COLOR TEST PAGE

You cannot run away from weakness;
you must some time fight it out or perish.
And if that be so, why not now and where you stand?
—Robert Louis Stevenson

1

1. Today, relax.
2. Take a deep breath in through your nose.
3. Hold it for three seconds.
4. Let it out through your mouth.
5. Then pull your shoulders down away from your ears.
6. Repeat five times.
7. Massage your temples & the back of your neck.
8. Repeat often, especially every time you feel fear rising up inside you.

2

1. Today, know that you are not alone.
2. You may feel alone. You may feel like everyone else is moving forward while you are stuck in one spot, trapped in fear.
3. But know this: fear is the number one reason that people fail to achieve their hopes, goals, & dreams. Simple, ordinary fear.
4. So don't be so hard on yourself.
5. Remind yourself that you're not alone, that you are in fact in excellent company with the rest of us who get afraid, as often as needed.

Breathe deeply in through your nose, hold briefly, let it out your mouth.

3

1. Today, reassure yourself.
2. Write the answer to this: *What supportive words do I most need to hear right now?*
3. Now look yourself in the eyes in a mirror & say those words aloud.
4. Then tell yourself that it's all going to be okay.
5. Because in the end, both it & you will be. And if, right now, it &/or you are not okay, that's simply because it's not the end yet.
6. Repeat whenever you feel fear rising inside you.

Breathe deeply in through your nose, hold briefly, let it out your mouth.

4
1. Today, face your fears.
2. Write a list of everything that makes you fearful (or worried/anxious/nervous, since those are all fear too, just dressed up as something else).
3. Read through your list.
4. Add any other fears you may have forgotten.

Breathe deeply. Reassure yourself with words you most need to hear.

5

1. Today, realize that not all fear is created equal.
2. Reorder your Day 4 list of fears from biggest fear to smallest fear.
3. For each one, answer this: *Is this fear something that could endanger my life (causing bodily injury or even my death)?*
4. Write the answer (*yes* or *no*) next to each.
5. Know this: real fear, I say kindly, consists only of those things that will endanger your life by pursuing them. That means all the *no* answers are just head fears that may *feel* real but, in truth, are simply in your mind.

Breathe deeply. Reassure yourself with words you most need to hear.

1. Today, be honest.
2. Read through the list of fears from Day 5. Circle the one with a *no* beside it (so a head fear) that matters deeply to you & also scares you the most.
3. In your mind, envision yourself stepping out & following that fear all the way to its end. Write down everything that scares you about pursuing that fear. Be specific. Write an answer to these: *What bad things do I think could come to pass if I go in the direction of that fear? What do I see as the worst possible outcome? What's the most horrible thing I imagine happening if I pursue that fear?*

Breathe deeply. Reassure yourself with words you most need to hear.

7

1. Today, think positive.
2. Start with the fear you circled on Day 6.
3. In your mind, envision yourself stepping out & following that fear all the way to its end. Write down everything good that could come from pursuing that fear. Be specific.
4. Write an answer to these: *What amazing things could come to pass in my life if I go in the direction of that fear? What do I see as the best possible outcome? What's the most phenomenal thing I imagine happening if I pursue that fear?*

Breathe deeply. Reassure yourself with words you most need to hear.

8

1. Today, say *yes*.
2. Look at your biggest head fear (the one you circled) from Day 6.
3. Say *yes* to that fear (because if you say *no*, your journey down that path ends).
4. Write your best possible outcome from Day 7 at the top of a new page.
5. Then work your way backward from that point to now.
6. Write all the actions you can think of that you'll have to take to get yourself from where you are now to that best outcome. If any action scares you, break it down into smaller & smaller (tiny, if need be) steps until it doesn't.

Breathe deeply. Reassure yourself with words you most need to hear.

9

1. Today, start walking through the fear.
2. Look at your list of steps from Day 8.
3. Take a deep breath in through your nose, hold it for three seconds, let it out through your mouth. Repeat (repeat, repeat) often.
4. Remember this: always aim for progress, not perfection. You'll conquer the fear if you'll just keep moving through it, if you'll just carry on.
5. Now take the first action on your list.

Breathe deeply. Reassure yourself with words you most need to hear.

10

1. Today, train your brain.
2. Read through your list from Day 5. Think about stepping out to do each one. Sit with all those feelings of fear & *really feel* the fear for 2 minutes. Don't do anything to numb or block or avoid the fear. Pay attention to how your body feels/reacts to fear, especially any differences between real fears & head fears.
3. Take note: you're still alive; nothing bad happened to you by feeling the fear.
4. This exercise helps train your brain to distinguish between real fear & head fear. That'll make it easier for you to push through head fears & move forward.

Breathe deeply, reassure yourself, take the next action on your Day 8 list.

11

1. Today, change the story you believe.
2. Read through the bad things & worst outcome you wrote on Day 6.
3. Know this: that is the story you're telling yourself about your head fear. You will believe (& so live out) whatever story you tell yourself over & over. But a story doesn't make that outcome true.
4. Answer this: *Will my self-worth & value still be intact no matter the end result?* (Hint: the answer is *yes*.)
5. Remember that whenever head fear rises up in you.

Breathe deeply, reassure yourself, take the next action on your Day 8 list.

12

1. Today, listen for the voice of wisdom inside you (your intuition).
2. Your intuition will never tear you down or berate you. Instead, it'll strengthen you & encourage you & help you grow. So be alone for 15 minutes.
3. Listen to that voice of wisdom & question your fears like: *If I wasn't afraid, what would I most want to have/be/do/say? If fear didn't stop me, where would I most want to go from here? Is it fear or truth that I speak to myself most often?*
4. Pick out any thoughts that build you up, motivate, &/or inspire you. Read them aloud. Repeat them whenever you feel head fear.

Breathe deeply, reassure yourself, take the next action on your Day 8 list.

13

1. Today, befriend yourself.
2. Write a kind letter to yourself, speaking strength to yourself & telling yourself what you most need to hear. Tell yourself things like: *I am intelligent, courageous, tenacious, determined, persistent,* etcetera.
3. Then write this: *I have nothing to fear. I am capable & strong enough to handle whatever comes my way. I will be victorious over my head fears.*
4. Find a mirror & look yourself in the eyes. Read that letter aloud.
5. Repeat often until those things become what you believe about yourself.

Breathe deeply, reassure yourself, take the next action on your Day 8 list.

14

1. Today, change how you look at risk.
2. Know this: security is an illusion. There are no absolute guarantees of either safety or comfort in nature. Avoiding fears that are in your head may make you *feel* safe but will not actually *keep* you safe.
3. So write this note: *Not pursuing my head fear(s) will not guarantee that I will be safe.* Now read your list from Day 5.
4. Then write this note: *Since there are no guarantees of safety or comfort, I might as well pursue those things that are head fears even if I have to do them afraid.*

Breathe deeply, reassure yourself, take the next action on your Day 8 list.

15

1. Today, change how you look at fear.
2. Knowing that security is an illusion, consider this: your head fear is actually a way for you to know in which direction you're supposed to be going.
3. Now take a look at your list from Day 5. Rewrite that list so it only includes those things with a *no* beside them *that matter the most to you*.
4. Let that list be what guides you from now on. Make what scares you into a road map to the life you most want.

Breathe deeply, reassure yourself, take the next action on your Day 8 list.

16

1. Today, check your motivation.
2. Read through your list from Day 15.
3. For each one, ask this: *Is achieving this something that deeply matters to me?* Write the answer (*yes* or *no*) next to each. Use your desire to achieve those things that deeply matter to you as fuel to move yourself through the fear.
4. When you make yourself (your own goals/dreams/passions) your sole motivation for achieving what you most want, the fear decreases because your actions become about fulfilling yourself & not about anything else.

Breathe deeply, reassure yourself, take the next action on your Day 8 list.

17

1. Today, enjoy yourself.
2. Write a list of things you love to do, things that light a spark in you, things that bring you joy & make you feel alive.
3. Pick one & do it today.
4. Let loose for a little while. Take your mind off everything.
5. Have fun!
6. Repeat often.

Breathe deeply, reassure yourself, take the next action on your Day 8 list.

18

1. Today, change how you look at life.
2. Choose to look at your entire life as a game or a big experiment. If you're playing a game & you lose, no big deal. Just play again. If you try something & it doesn't work, no big deal. Just try again.
3. Now decide to lower the stakes & take the pressure off. Remember: your self-worth & value are always intact no matter what. So have the mindset that you're simply going to move forward & see what works & what doesn't.
4. Choose (yes, it's a choice) to have fun while you're figuring out your life.

Breathe deeply, reassure yourself, take the next action on your Day 8 list.

19

1. Today, stop believing in failure.
2. You will *always* live out what you believe. So choose (yes, it's a choice, I say kindly) to stop believing in failure. Instead, start believing that there are only two outcomes when you make choices/take action: either success or learning.
3. Write this: *I believe there is only success or learning. Only success or learning.*
4. Then make that the foundation upon which you build your life.
5. Make that your mantra & repeat often, especially when fear keeps you from taking action & moving forward in your life.

Breathe deeply, reassure yourself, take the next action on your Day 8 list.

20

1. Today, let go.
2. Write a list of things you are hanging on to that are fueling your fear (like: the outcome, other people's opinions/wishes/expectations, numbers/rankings/statistics of any kind, your own insecurities about not being enough/ready/experienced, any excuses why you can't, etcetera.)
3. Choose (yes, it's a choice) to let all that go. None of it matters.
4. Remember: you are moving through the fear *for you & you alone* (see Day 16), so you can have the life you most want.

Breathe deeply, reassure yourself, take the next action on your Day 8 list.

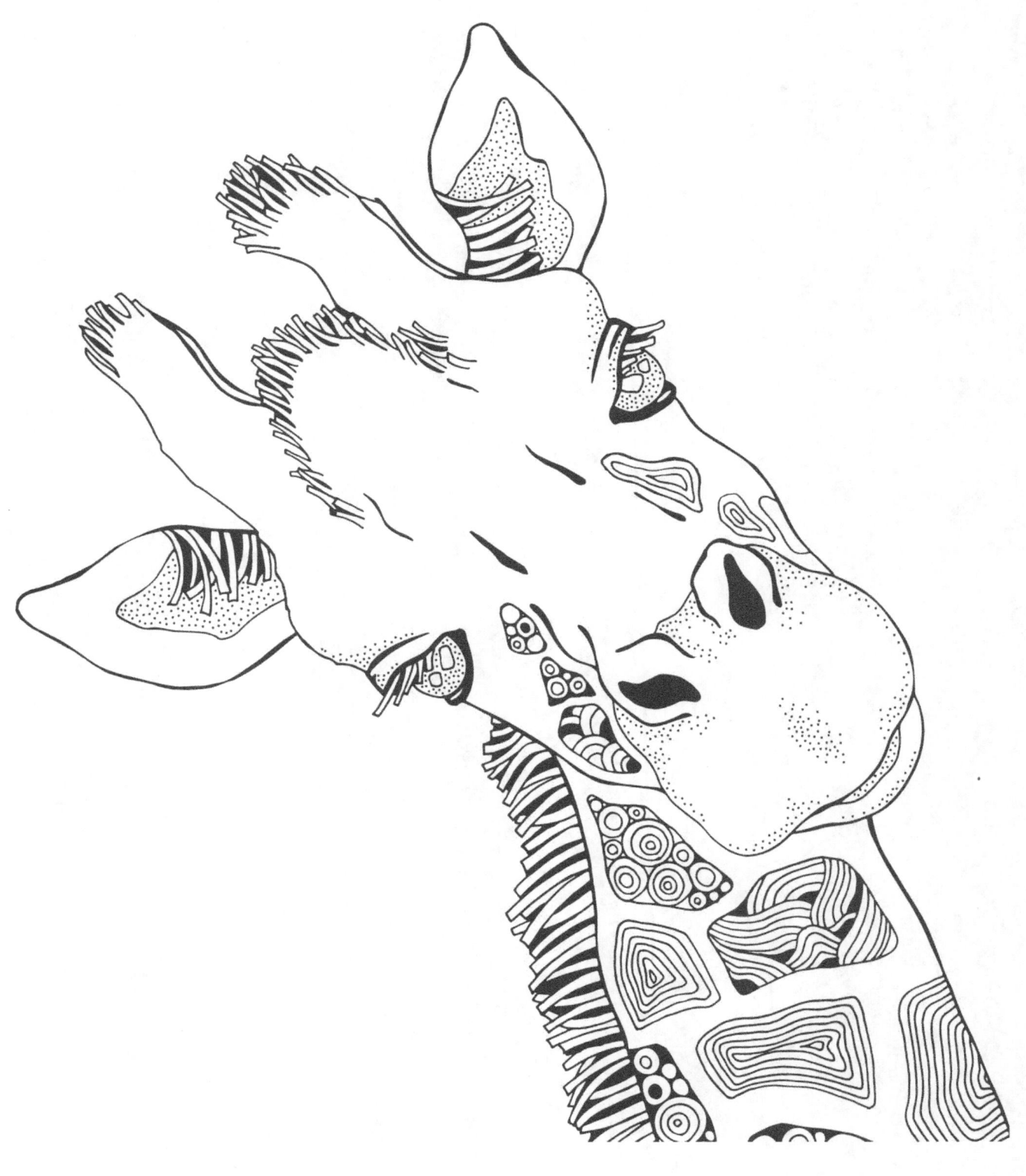

21

1. Today, acknowledge your own strength & courage.
2. Be proud of yourself for moving forward in the direction of your fears.
3. Buy/give yourself a little (or big) something you really want as a reward.
4. Then take a look at your list from Day 17.
5. Pick something & go do it.
6. Have fun!

Breathe deeply, reassure yourself, take the next action on your Day 8 list.

22

1. Today, choose an easier path.
2. Your fear may feel like a mountain you are trying to climb.
3. Know this: you get to choose just how steep that mountain is, which means you can make it a gently-sloping hill or you can make it Mount Everest. Manageable or overwhelming: it's all in how you choose to look at it.
4. Write how you can make moving forward through the fear an easy path that you can enjoy along the way. (Hint: make the steps smaller, take time to relax, delegate things you don't like to do, give yourself rewards, etcetera.)

Breathe deeply, reassure yourself, take the next action on your Day 8 list.

23

1. Today, befriend yourself again.
2. Reread your letter to yourself from Day 13.
3. Now write an addition to that letter about how proud you are of yourself, how far you've come, that you felt scared but kept moving forward anyway, that your aim is always progress & not perfection, that you are indeed strong, courageous, & fully capable of achieving whatever you want in life.
4. Look yourself in the eyes in a mirror. Read that letter aloud. Then say those things over & over until they become the story you believe about yourself.

Breathe deeply, reassure yourself, take the next action on your Day 8 list.

24

1. Today, promise yourself.
2. Know this: at some point you're going to want to quit. So choose today, before you're tempted, what you will do when the temptation comes.
3. Write an unbreakable promise to yourself: *I will press on no matter what may get thrown at me. I will keep moving through the fear.*
4. Then also add that promise to the bottom of your letter from Day 23.
5. Now have integrity & keep your word to your own self. You're worth the effort.

Breathe deeply, reassure yourself, take the next action on your Day 8 list.

25

1. Today, take heart.
2. Know this: the *only* difference between those who succeed & those who fail is that the former group doesn't let their mistakes derail them. Mistakes are simply a brand new chance to do it better the next time, to come at it again with more wisdom & perspective.
3. Write a list of mistakes you've made & what you've learned from them.
4. Let that list strengthen you & fuel you to succeed on your next try.
5. Remember your mantra: *I believe there is only success or learning.*

Breathe deeply, reassure yourself, take the next action on your Day 8 list.

26

1. Today, look in the direction you're going.
2. So don't look back & hang on to your history or look around & compare yourself with what others are doing.
3. Instead look forward to where you want to be.
4. Now write this: *My journey is my own. I do what I do because it deeply matters to me & that's reason enough. I have nothing to prove to anyone but myself.*
5. Then look yourself in the eyes in a mirror & read that aloud. Believe it.
6. Know this: the fear will decrease when you believe those truths.

Breathe deeply, reassure yourself, take the next action on your Day 8 list.

27

1. Today, keep saying *yes* (because, remember, if you say *no*, your journey down that path ends).
2. Write this: *I say yes to those things that are head fears. I choose to believe that life is on my side, has my back, & that everything, in the end, works in my favor. I will always choose to believe that something good is coming my way.*
3. Now take a look at the list you wrote on Day 15.
4. Say *yes* to all of those things that deeply matter to you even if they scare you because there will be something amazing at the end of each one.

Breathe deeply, reassure yourself, take the next action on your Day 8 list.

28

1. Today, empower yourself.
2. Write an answer to this: *What holds the ultimate power over me & my life, is it me or is it my fear?*
3. Choose to see fear as a prison you have put yourself in & only you have the key to let yourself out. That key is simply changing your mind. Choose, *right now & where you stand,* to believe that pursuing your head fears will help you grow into the person you want to be & the person you are meant to be.
4. So embrace your journey, keep taking action, & claim your power back.

Breathe deeply, reassure yourself, take the next action on your Day 8 list.

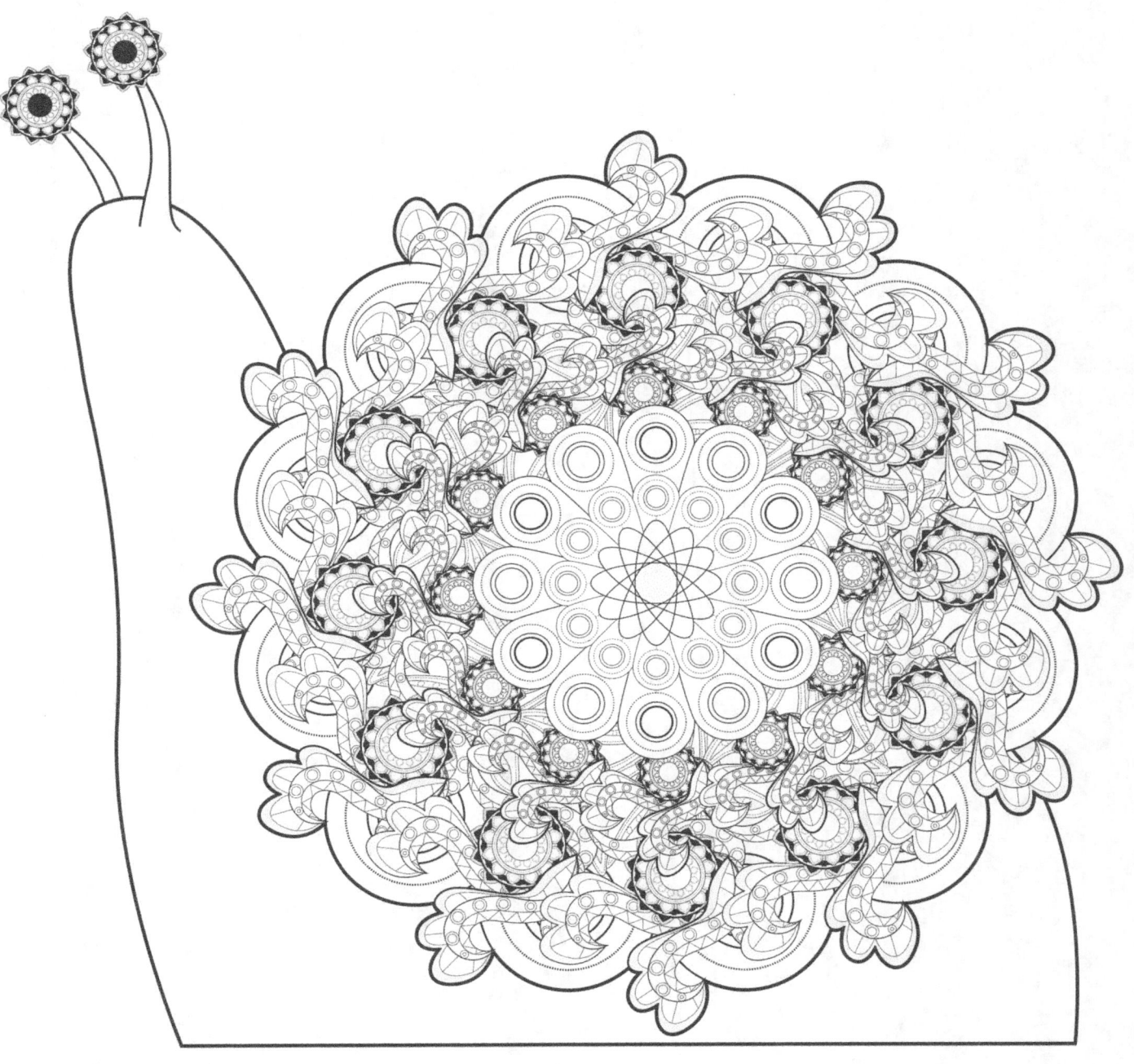

29

1. Today, be willing to grow slowly.
2. Know this: it doesn't matter *in the least* how slowly you're moving as long as you keep moving in the direction you most want to go & you don't stop.
3. Reread your unbreakable promise from Day 24.
4. Write another unbreakable promise to add to it: *I may go slowly, but I won't stop.* Reread whenever you need a reminder to keep going.
5. Keep taking action *every day* until you reach that best outcome from Day 7. If you keep moving forward, you'll get there. You will.

Breathe deeply, reassure yourself, take the next action on your Day 8 list.

30

1. Today, celebrate!
2. Be proud of yourself for how far you've come.
3. Write down your successes & victories (big or small).
4. Do something nice for yourself (like a prize for a job well done).
5. Go & enjoy your life!

Breathe deeply, reassure yourself, take the next action on your Day 8 list.

ABOUT THE AUTHOR!

This book was born out of Shelli Johnson's own struggle with fear. She wanted and needed to heal herself. She wanted and needed practical and easy steps she could take to move through the fear so she could stop being stuck and start having the life she most wanted. So she simply wrote the book she needed to read. Every day, she does her best to cut herself some slack & practice progress, not perfection.

Shelli's also an award-winning journalist (sports reporting), novelist (grand prize winner), and blogger (shellijohnson.com/blog). She's a truck owner, horse rider, photographer, yoga enthusiast, and slow-cooker fan (shellijohnson.com/recipes). Find out more at: shellijohnson.com/about

**Find out about Shelli's other books at:
shellijohnson.com/books**

GET YOUR FREE STUFF!

Visit: shellijohnson.com/signup
Opt-in for the newsletter to keep in touch.
Get a free bookmark to color.

ACKNOWLEDGMENTS!

My sincere thanks to people who make my days brighter:
Rollin Johnson
Heather Porazzo

Disclosures and Disclaimers

This book is published in print format. All trademarks and service marks are the properties of their respective owners. All references to these properties are made solely for editorial purposes. Except for marks actually owned by the Author or the Publisher, no commercial claims are made to their use, and neither the Author nor the Publisher is affiliated with such marks in any way.

Unless otherwise expressly noted, none of the individuals or business entities mentioned herein has endorsed the contents of this book.

Limits of Liability & Disclaimers of Warranties
Because this book is a general educational information product, it is not a substitute for professional advice on the topics discussed in it.

The materials in this book are provided "as is" and without warranties of any kind either express or implied. The Author and the Publisher disclaim all warranties, express or implied, including, but not limited to, implied warranties of merchantability and fitness for a particular purpose. The Author and the Publisher do not warrant that defects will be corrected. The Author does not warrant or make any representations regarding the use or the results of the use of the materials in this book in terms of their correctness, accuracy, reliability, or otherwise. Applicable law may not allow the exclusion of implied warranties, so the above exclusion may not apply to you.

Under no circumstances, including, but not limited to, negligence, shall the Author or the Publisher be liable for any special or consequential damages that result from the use of, or the inability to use this book, even if the Author, the Publisher, or an authorized representative has been advised of the possibility of such damages. Applicable law may not allow the limitation or exclusion of liability or incidental or consequential damages, so the above limitation or exclusion may not apply to you. In no event shall the Author or Publisher total liability to you for all damages, losses, and causes of action (whether in contract, tort, including but not limited to, negligence or otherwise) exceed the amount paid by you, if any, for this book.

You agree to hold the Author and the Publisher of this book, principals, agents, affiliates, and employees harmless from any and all liability for all claims for damages due to injuries, including attorney fees and costs, incurred by you or caused to third parties by you, arising out of the products, services, and activities discussed in this book, excepting only claims for gross negligence or intentional tort.

You agree that any and all claims for gross negligence or intentional tort shall be settled solely by confidential binding arbitration per the American Arbitration Association's commercial arbitration rules. Your claim cannot be aggregated with third party claims. All arbitration must occur in the municipality where the Author's principal place of business is located. Arbitration fees and costs shall be split equally, and you are solely responsible for your own lawyer fees.

Facts and information are believed to be accurate at the time they were placed in this book. All data provided in this book is to be used for information purposes only. The information contained within is not intended to provide specific legal, financial, tax, physical or mental health advice, or any other advice whatsoever, for any individual or company and should not be relied upon in that regard. The services described are only offered in jurisdictions where they may be legally offered. Information provided is not all-inclusive, and is limited to information that is made available and such information should not be relied upon as all-inclusive or accurate.

For more information about this policy, please contact the Author at the website address listed in the Copyright Notice at the front of this book.

IF YOU DO NOT AGREE WITH THESE TERMS AND EXPRESS CONDITIONS, DO NOT READ THIS BOOK. YOUR USE OF THIS BOOK, INCLUDING PRODUCTS, SERVICES, AND ANY PARTICIPATION IN ACTIVITIES MENTIONED IN THIS BOOK, MEAN THAT YOU ARE AGREEING TO BE LEGALLY BOUND BY THESE TERMS.

Affiliate Compensation & Material Connections Disclosure
This book may contain references to websites and information created and maintained by other individuals and organizations. The Author and the Publisher do not control or guarantee the accuracy, completeness, relevance, or timeliness of any information or privacy policies posted on these websites.

You should assume that all references to products and services in this book are made because material connections exist between the Author or Publisher and the providers of the mentioned products and services ("Provider"). You should also assume that all website links within this book are affiliate links for (a) the Author, (b) the Publisher, or (c) someone else who is an affiliate for the mentioned products and services (individually and collectively, the "Affiliate").

The Affiliate recommends products and services in this book based in part on a good faith belief that the purchase of such products or services will help readers in general.

The Affiliate has this good faith belief because (a) the Affiliate has tried the product or service mentioned prior to recommending it or (b) the Affiliate has researched the reputation of the Provider and has made the decision to recommend the Provider's products or services based on the Provider's history of providing these or other products or services.

The representations made by the Affiliate about products and services reflect the Affiliate's honest opinion based upon the facts known to the Affiliate at the time this book was published.

Because there is a material connection between the Affiliate and Providers of products or services mentioned in this book, you should always assume that the Affiliate may be biased because of the Affiliate's relationship with a Provider and/or because the Affiliate has received or will receive something of value from a Provider.

Perform your own due diligence before purchasing a product or service mentioned in this book.

The type of compensation received by the Affiliate may vary. In some instances, the Affiliate may receive complimentary products (such as a review copy), services, or money from a Provider prior to mentioning the Provider's products or services in this book.

In addition, the Affiliate may receive a monetary commission or non-monetary compensation when you take action by using a website link within in this book. This includes, but is not limited to, when you purchase a product or service from a Provider after going to a website link contained in this book.

Health Disclaimers
As an express condition to reading to this book, you understand and agree to the following terms.

This book is a general educational health-related information product. This book does not contain medical advice.

The book's content is not a substitute for direct, personal, professional medical care and diagnosis. None of the exercises or treatments (including products and services) mentioned in this book should be performed or otherwise used without prior approval from your physician or other qualified professional health care provider.

There may be risks associated with participating in activities or using products and services mentioned in this book for people in poor health or with pre-existing physical or mental health conditions.

Because these risks exist, you will not use such products or participate in such activities if you are in poor health or have a pre-existing mental or physical condition. If you choose to participate in these risks, you do so of your own free will and accord, knowingly and voluntarily assuming all risks associated with such activities.

Earnings & Income Disclaimers
No Earnings Projections, Promises or Representations

For purposes of these disclaimers, the term "Author" refers individually and collectively to the author of this book and to the affiliate (if any) whose affiliate hyperlinks are referenced in this book.

You recognize and agree that the Author and the Publisher have made no implications, warranties, promises, suggestions, projections, representations or guarantees whatsoever to you about future prospects or earnings, or that you will earn any money, with respect to your purchase of this book, and that the Author and the Publisher have not authorized any such projection, promise, or representation by others.

Any earnings or income statements, or any earnings or income examples, are only estimates of what you might earn. There is no assurance you will do as well as stated in any examples. If you rely upon any figures provided, you must accept the entire risk of not doing as well as the information provided. This applies whether the earnings or income examples are monetary in nature or pertain to advertising credits which may be earned (whether such credits are convertible to cash or not).

There is no assurance that any prior successes or past results as to earnings or income (whether monetary or advertising credits, whether convertible to cash or not) will apply, nor can any prior successes be used, as an indication of your future success or results from any of the information, content, or strategies. Any and all claims or representations as to income or earnings (whether monetary or advertising credits, whether convertible to cash or not) are not to be considered as "average earnings".

Testimonials & Examples

Testimonials and examples in this book are exceptional results, do not reflect the typical purchaser's experience, do not apply to the average person and are not intended to represent or guarantee that anyone will achieve the same or similar results. Where specific income or earnings (whether monetary or advertising credits, whether convertible to cash or not), figures are used and attributed to a specific individual or business, that individual or business has earned that amount. There is no assurance that you will do as well using the same information or strategies. If you rely on the specific income or earnings figures used, you must accept all the risk of not doing as well. The described experiences are atypical. Your financial results are likely to differ from those described in the testimonials.

The Economy

The economy, where you do business, on a national and even worldwide scale, creates additional uncertainty and economic risk. An economic recession or depression might negatively affect your results.

Your Success or Lack of It

Your success in using the information or strategies provided in this book depends on a variety of factors. The Author and the Publisher have no way of knowing how well you will do because they do not know you, your background, your work ethic, your dedication, your motivation, your desire, or your business skills or practices. Therefore, neither the Author nor the Publisher guarantees or implies that you will get rich, that you will do as well, or that you will have any earnings (whether monetary or advertising credits, whether convertible to cash or not), at all.

Businesses and earnings derived therefrom involve unknown risks and are not suitable for everyone. You may not rely on any information presented in this book or otherwise provided by the Author or the Publisher, unless you do so with the knowledge and understanding that you can experience significant losses (including, but not limited to, the loss of any monies paid to purchase this book and/or any monies spent setting up, operating, and/or marketing your business activities, and further, that you may have no earnings at all (whether monetary or advertising credits, whether convertible to cash or not).

Forward-Looking Statements

Materials in this book may contain information that includes or is based upon forward-looking statements within the meaning of the Securities Litigation Reform Act of 1995. Forward-looking statements give the Author's expectations or forecasts of future events. You can identify these statements by the fact that they do not relate strictly to historical or current facts. They use words such as "anticipate," "estimate," "expect," "project," "intend," "plan," "believe," and other words and terms of similar meaning in connection with a description of potential earnings or financial performance.

Any and all forward looking statements here or on any materials in this book are intended to express an opinion of earnings potential. Many factors will be important in determining your actual results and no guarantees are made that you will achieve results similar to the Author or anybody else. In fact, no guarantees are made that you will achieve any results from applying the Author's ideas, strategies, and tactics found in this book.

Purchase Price

Although the Publisher believes the price is fair for the value that you receive, you understand and agree that the purchase price for this book has been arbitrarily set by the Publisher or the vendor who sold you this book. This price bears no relationship to objective standards.

Due Diligence

You are advised to do your own due diligence when it comes to making any decisions. Use caution and seek the advice of qualified professionals before acting upon the contents of this book or any other information. You shall not consider any examples, documents, or other content in this book or otherwise provided by the Author or Publisher to be the equivalent of professional advice.

The Author and the Publisher assume no responsibility for any losses or damages resulting from your use of any link, information, or opportunity contained in this book or within any other information disclosed by the Author or the Publisher in any form whatsoever.

YOU SHOULD ALWAYS CONDUCT YOUR OWN INVESTIGATION (PERFORM DUE DILIGENCE)
BEFORE BUYING PRODUCTS OR SERVICES FROM ANYONE. THIS INCLUDES PRODUCTS AND SERVICES
SOLD VIA WEBSITE LINKS REFERENCED IN THIS BOOK.

www.ingramcontent.com/pod-product-compliance
Lightning Source LLC
Chambersburg PA
CBHW060515300426
44112CB00017B/2686